Beyond Sodom:

Has America Lost God's Smiles?

Aaron B. Claxton, PhD

Beyond Sodom: Has America Lost God's Smiles?

Copyright © 2016 by Aaron B. Claxton, PhD

All rights reserved. No part of this book may be reproduced, stored in retrieval system or transmitted in any form or by any means – electronic, mechanical, photocopy, recording or otherwise – except for brief quotations in printed reviews, without the prior written permission of the author.

Unless otherwise indicated, all Scripture is quoted from the King James Version of the Holy Bible.

Kingdom Kaught Publishing, LLC
Denton, Maryland

Printed in the U.S.A.

ISBN: 978-0-9964040-4-4

DEDICATION

It gives me great pleasure to dedicate this book to my beloved and indispensable wife, of over 58 years. She is not only my lover, and confidante, but also my helper, critic and encourager in everything I do, including this book.

She is forever my proofreader, advisor and all that I have ever needed in this business of book writing. Dr. Deborah J. Claxton has earned several degrees and has of late received her doctorate of Religious Education and is an author in her own right. Thank God for "Dr. Deborah," as she is affectionately known by many, and "Sugar Lump," as she is known by me.

Beyond Sodom: Has America Lost God's Smiles?

At the very inception of the United States of America, the father of our nation prayed a prayer of dedication over America. That prayer was prayed at St. Paul's Chapel located right at "ground zero" in New York City. President George Washington called upon the Father of our Lord Jesus Christ, whom he addressed as "Providence," and asked Him to bless this fledgling nation above all other nations based on Psalm 33:12. That Psalm says: "Blessed is the nation whose God is the LORD (Yahweh)". George Washington concluded his prayer by saying, "But if this nation (America) ever turns its back on God, it would lose God's smiles (or favor). President Abraham Lincoln also prayed (in effect) to "Let not this nation think that it has secured its bountiful blessings by its own strength, but rather by the blessings of Almighty God."

Grateful Americans ought to give Jehovah honor as Lord over America! We have written and sung songs like "God Bless America," etc., yet America has dishonored God in its public policies, laws and practices, on an ever increasing basis! Roe vs. Wade which was endorsed by our Supreme Court in 1973, wherein the top Justices in the land, declared that death to the unborn was okay! However, God on the other hand, has said "Choose life, that both you and your descendants may live" (Deut. 30:19b).

The title of this book is "BEYOND SODOM: HAS AMERICA LOST GOD'S SMILES"?

Based on the observations I have made during my nearly 82 year journey on earth and in America, I would venture to say that America has indeed begun to lose God's smiles and protections. America has far exceeded Sodom and Gomorrah in its wickedness, yea sexual perversions! The Sodomites simply practiced unnatural sex called homosexuality or lesbianism! The LORD displayed His great displeasure by pouring out destruction upon them in the form of fire and brimstone (Gen. 19:24). The Lord also seriously condemned the above mentioned sexual misbehavior by calling it an abomination (something God abhors) (Lev. 18:22).

Aaron B. Claxton, PhD

Our Supreme Court, on June 26, 2015, did the unthinkable in the world's leading "Christian" nation, the United States of America, by endorsing same sex "marriage" as the law of the land! 51% of Americans approve what the Bible calls wickedness (perversion) and an abomination (that which God hates passionately)! The Supreme Court's approval and legalization of same sex "marriage" defiles and corrupts the oldest human institution on Earth, and insults and infuriates the God who initiated the same! Listen to the word of God:

> "...in the image of God He created him (mankind); male and female. He created them. Then God blessed them, and God said to them, 'Be fruitful and multiply; fill the earth and subdue it'" (Gen 27:28).

Additionally, let us hear the words of Jesus Christ the Son of God - God himself in human flesh:

> "And he answered and said to them, 'Have you not read that He who made them at the beginning made them male

and female,' and said, 'For this reason a man shall leave his father and mother and be joined to his wife (a woman), and the two shall become one flesh'? So then they are no longer two but one flesh" (Matt. 19:4-6; Gen 2:24).

After God's destruction of Sodom and Gomorrah by fire, Lot's two daughters got him drunk and had sex with him so that they could have children. This was incest and certainly frowned upon by God. However, the daughters reasoned thusly:

> "Now the firstborn (daughter) said to the younger, 'Our father is old and there is no man on the earth to come in to us as is the custom of all the earth'" (Gen.19:31).

So we say boldly, according to the Bible and human science, there is no way humanly possible for people of the same sex to produce children! In no way can people of the same sex fulfill God's mandate to "be fruitful and multiply; fill the earth…" (Gen 1:28). Oh sure, they can and do adopt unsuspecting and helpless children, and corrupt them with their abominable practices! They will answer to God for their wickedness.

These people call their same sexual perversion "love." No sir! That's not love. It is lust! God's word says: "But each one is tempted when he (or she) is drawn away by his (or her) own desires and enticed. Then when desire (lust) is conceived, it gives birth to sin; and sin, when it is full grown brings forth death. Do not be deceived… (James 1:14-16). These "same-sexers" are deceived by the same deceiver who tempted and deceived Eve in the garden (Genesis 3:1-7).

The Apostle Paul wrote to Christians at Corinth, (often called the "Hell hole of the Mediterranean") and said, "For I am jealous for you with godly jealousy. For I have betrothed you to one husband, that I may present you as a chaste virgin to Christ. But I fear lest somehow, as the serpent deceived Eve by his craftiness, so your minds may be corrupted from the simplicity (the purity) that is in Christ" (1 Corinthians 11:2-3). Same-sex "marriage" thinking is inimical to the purity of Bible marriage, which God originally intended, and designed it for marriage between one man and one woman!

Jehovah God, the God of creation, Israel, the church and America, is a God of order and design! He designed human marriage to be lived out in a home consisting of a father (a male husband) a mother (a female wife) and children of both sexes. That was his original plan, order and design. Anything less than this is a hoax and a fraud, a misrepresentation! It is twisted and perverse!

In Psalm 82, we find the Lord God Almighty rebuking the judges of Israel (like our Supreme Court justices) by saying "How long will you judge unjustly, and show partiality to the wicked (the perverse)? ...They do not know, nor do they understand; they walk about in darkness; all the foundations of the earth (and our Nation and society) are out of course" (Psalms 82:2, 5). The psalmist asks the question in another place, "If the foundations are destroyed, what can the righteous do"? (Psalms 11:3).

What then is in store for America? The walls of protection by which God has protected this favored land will soon be penetrated and torn down. Why would one say this? Because America's God is a God of consistency and longsuffering. God has borne with America for many years-229 years to be exact! The average life span of a nation is 200 years! We have exceeded that average by twenty nine years! The more of God's goodness and mercy He has bestowed on America, the more we have rebelled against Him; and have counted His word and His church ("the pillar and ground of the truth") as a joke - something to mock and at which to poke fun. This nation has forgotten God and the biblical precepts upon which it was built! It has forgotten that America was established as "the land of the free and the home of the brave" - a kind of a "Promised Land," like Israel.

Most of America does not know that this nation was declared to be "A Christian Nation" by the Supreme Court case called the "Trinity Case," in 1898! Psalm 9:17 says: "The wicked (the perverse) shall be turned into hell, and all those nations that forget God." Most Americans have no knowledge of the Mayflower Compact wherein Christian believers from England dedicated this land to God and the Lord Jesus Christ in the 1600's, in Jamestown, Virginia. They committed themselves to proclaiming the Gospel of Jesus Christ throughout this land. Most Americans do not know that the Protestant believers from Holland, England and other European countries fled from Europe because of persecution and oppression, to have freedom of expression of their Christian faith!

One of the principal foundations of America is liberty! That is, freedom of conscience, freedom of speech, freedom of assembly, freedom of worship and other freedoms. These freedoms were at the root of this nation's laws and Constitution, and were birthed out of the Protestant Christian faith! The founders were following precepts of the Hebrew faith. The freedoms bequeathed to America by its founders were not freedoms to oppose nor insult the righteousness and holiness of God! The freedoms that the founders fought for did not include libertinism nor licentiousness! God is holy and He wants this land to be clean and holy! The Lord warned Israel in the Old Testament against sexual perversion, i.e. sodomy and bestiality. God said, "Do not defile yourselves in any of these ways; because this is how even the land (the earth in that land) was defiled; so I punished it for its sin, and the land vomited out its inhabitants… And if you defile or (pollute) the land, it will vomit you out as it vomited out the nations that were before you" (Lev. 18:24-28).

It is my biblically based conviction that America has gone beyond the point of no return, in that America has exceeded the sins of Sodom and Gomorrah in its attempt to redefine marriage! God has been exceedingly patient with America, but America has gotten worse! Solomon who is called, "the preacher," in his biblical book called, Proverbs, warns:

> "He who is often reproved and hardens (or stiffens) his neck will be cut off (destroyed) suddenly, and that without remedy" (Prov. 29:1).

Listen to the Prophet Isaiah's words to backslidden Israel, as I apply those words to America: "Ah, sinful nation, a people loaded with guilt, a brood of evildoers, children given to corruption! They have forsaken the LORD; they have spurned the Holy One of Israel and turned their backs on him…When you spread out your hands in prayer, I will hide my eyes from you; even if you offer prayers, I will not listen. Your hands are full of blood; (The Supreme Court sanctioned abortion in

1973), wash and make yourselves clean. Take your evil deeds out of my sight! Stop doing wrong..." (Isaiah 1:4, 15-16).

It is reported that President Barack Obama is the most abortion-sanctioning and homosexual-approving President in the history of America! The Lord Jesus Christ wept over Jerusalem just as He has been weeping over America. And He finally pronounced judgment on Jerusalem, as He will do on backsliding America. Christ's words of judgment are as follows: "O Jerusalem, Jerusalem...how often have I longed to gather your children together, as a hen gathers her chicks under her wings, but you were not willing (You have done worse and worse). Look, your house is left to you desolate" (Matthew 23:37, NIV).

There are those who are saying that the Muslim Radicals will not penetrate our security defenses and destroy America. Well they did on 9/11! But only to a small degree. However, since American leadership and 51% of our population have endorsed even greater wickedness (same-sex "marriage"); God's nostrils can no longer tolerate the greater stench that has come up before Him since 911! While the timid or uninformed pulpits are saying: "Peace and safety, destruction will come on them suddenly, as labor pains on a pregnant woman, and they will not escape" (I Thessalonians 5:3).

Do I believe in prayer to invoke God's mercy? I say yes! A thousand times yes! But, I am also one of God's end-time prophetic apostles who perceives in the Spirit that God is saying "Enough is enough, and the end is at hand!" I cannot say how long it will take for foreign enemies to break through our defenses, but it will be sooner than many think! The Lord is long suffering and plenteous in mercy, but even His patience has a breaking point! This nation has sorely tested God's patience in America's embrace of homosexuality and same-sex lifestyles. We have totally overlooked the fact that God vehemently abhors homosexuality (Leviticus 18:22). How much more do you suppose He abhors and hates what Americans call "same-sex marriage"? This social aberration strikes at the very heart of the human family - the most ancient human social unit established by God Himself! (Genesis 27:28). Even the animals, the brute beasts, follow God's divine order. Male animals mate with female animals of the same species to produce offspring in that specie. They don't get confused like human kind, with males going after males and females going after females! The Apostle Paul explains to us by revelation from God that the homosexual condition came upon mankind basically because of pride and idolatry!

Apostle Paul wrote:

> "For the wrath of God is revealed from heaven against all ungodliness and unrighteousness of men, who suppress the truth in unrighteousness…because although they knew God, they did not glorify Him as God, nor were thankful, but became futile in their thoughts, and their foolish hearts were darkened. Professing themselves to be wise (the Greeks and Romans for example) they became fools, and changed the glory of the Incorruptible God into the likeness of perishable man and birds and four-footed animals and creeping things. Therefore, God also gave them up to uncleanness, in the lusts of their hearts to dishonor their bodies among themselves, who changed the truth of God for the lie, and wor-

shipped and served the creature rather than the Creator, who is blessed forever Amen. For this reason God gave them up to vile passions. For their women exchanged the natural use for what is against nature. Likewise also the men leaving the natural use of the woman, burned in their lust for one another, men with men committing what is shameful, and receiving in themselves the penalty of their error which was due. And even as they did not like to retain God in their knowledge, God gave them up to a debased mind, to do those things which are not fitting; being filled with all unrighteousness, sexual immortality, wickedness…who knowing the righteous judgment of God that those who practice such things are deserving of death, not only do the same, but also approve of those who practice them" (Romans 1:18-32).

It is sad to say that our current president, President Barack Obama, and his hopeful successor, former Secretary of State Hillary Clinton, openly and wholeheartedly endorse homosexuality and same sex "marriage"; while the Bible wholeheartedly condemns homosexuality as being worthy of God's unmitigated wrath! They simply count these filthy practices as a part of a "cultural change" or a "shift in social attitudes."

There are and have been leading liberal, national lawmakers who want to make it illegal in America for preachers to openly preach against homosexuality or same-sex "marriage" from their pulpits. They want to legally label such biblical preaching as "hate speech." It is sad to say that this already happened in Canada and Sweden, where Bible preachers have been jailed for this so-called "hate speech." God forbid that such legislation becomes the law In America! I personally believe that Apostle Paul's treatise on the wrath of God being revealed from Heaven against all manner of unrighteousness, especially homosexuality, is the greatest explanation ever written on the source, reason and expected end of homosexuality, and by the same token on same-sex "marriage!"

Why do I continue to say that America is on her way to destruction? Because the polls say that 51% of

Aaron B. Claxton, PhD

America publicly endorses the heinous sin of so-called same-sex "marriage!" The word of God says, *"Righteousness exalts a nation, but sin is a reproach to any people"* (Proverbs 14:34). I believe I can say with certainty that America has been blessed to be the head of nations because we had God-fearing, Bible-believing founding fathers, and many of our presidents and lawmakers were such. King Solomon, the richest and wisest king in human history declared:

> "When the righteous are in authority, the people rejoice; but when a wicked man rules, the people groan" (Proverbs 29:2).

Who can say for sure when America's demise will come? Nobody but God and His anointed prophets. Amos the prophet declared: "Surely the Lord God does nothing, unless He reveals His secret to His servants the prophets" (Amos 3:7). But as surely as the sun sets, the demise of America is coming because America through its recent administrations, and its current administration, has turned its back on God, by departing from His word and His ways! No one but God Himself, or one of His anointed prophets, can predict precisely when America's demise will come. We do know from history that America's presidents (many of them) and military leaders, recognized Jehovah as the only true God, and Christianity as God's true faith and religion. Some of America's presidents and leaders from Revolutionary times to the Korean Police Action equated Christianity with Democracy. We are keenly aware that from the 50's and 60's forward, America has experienced major social and cultural shifts away from Christian morality and godliness, toward a secular, non-religious world view.

George Orwell in his book, "1984" (written in the early '50's) attempted to foresee America in her "post glory days" – a nation of former glory having been destroyed and devastated by the "atomic bombs" of the Soviet Union. He "foresaw" a fallen United States of America, under the heel of Russia being watched by "Big Brother" on every corner. What George Orwell could not see is that by the late 80's or early 90's there would be no more Soviet Union! That godless system would be destroyed, and Russia would be divested of its former satellite states and glory.

On the other hand, Tom Brokaw, one of America's most esteemed television reporters and anchors, wrote a book upon retirement, about "America's Greatest Generation," which referenced the World War II generation as America's greatest. It was a time he said, "of strong patriotism and strong moral and Christian faith in America."

After that period America began its long social and spiritual decline. It turned from the Biblical faith and prayers of its earlier years to a secular culture, and an immoral culture, where anything base became acceptable! That's where America has ended up today! It is spiritually bankrupt! America's downward anti-biblical slide began with Dr. Kinsey's Report on human sexuality in America which promoted a sexual revolution in America. Then came the Women's Liberation movement resulting in the U.S. Supreme Court's ruling on abortion known as Roe vs. Wade. Women wanted more control over their own bodies, to abort babies at will. History shows that America was built on the Bible and its Christian teachings, i.e., from its inception. Most Americans guided their lives by the Bible. Regarding marriage, the Bible teaches the following:

> "The husband should fulfill his marital duty to his wife, and likewise the wife to the husband. The wife's body does not belong to her alone but also to her husband. In the same way, the husband's body does not belong to him alone but also to his wife" (1 Corinthians 7:4).

The social and sexual revolution in America was accompanied by a change in its musical tastes. "Be-Bop" was the music of the 50's, where getting high on drugs was the in-thing. I know, because I was a part of it until I was confronted with eternity and yielded my life to God in 1957, in salvation. After Be-Bop came the Beatles and Elvis Presley, with the "shaking of booties." Many American young people lost their innocence and virginity during that time. "Virgin" became a bad word.

During the 70's we saw the "Flower Power kids" who lived in communes in their rebellion against the "old social order." We also saw the open rebellion against all authority, the open use of drugs and the massive demonstrations against the Vietnam War.

Aaron B. Claxton, PhD

We must recognize however that the Civil Rights movement during the 50's and 60's was a good thing, where the conscience of America was pricked to bring about change in the treatment of African Americans. After all, these were the people who helped the Israelites in several Old Testament instances, and helped Jesus carry his cross. But on the heels of that Movement came the Women's Liberation Movement that gave rise to Roe vs Wade. That Supreme Court decision gave rise to the present day same sex "marriage" Supreme Court decision. This is closely being followed by the LGTB movement rising up and demanding its "rights".

Once again, we refer to Leviticus 18 which deals with God's Laws of Sexual Morality. Verse 29 of that Chapter tells us that Israel's land was defiled because of the abominations (sexual immoralities in particular) that had been committed by their predecessors (the Jebusites, the Hivites and other "ites"); and that which the Israelites had partaken of themselves. Just as *sexual immoralities* defiled and corrupted the land of Israel, so are the aforementioned *abominations* that have been endorsed by our United States Supreme Court, corrupting and defiling our beautiful land called America!

We repeat, America's founders and forefathers asked Jesus Christ to be Lord of this land that we call America. The Lord consented to their requests. But let us be reminded that Christ's Lordship over America carries with it certain responsibilities and consequences. Responsibilities: "Serve the Lord with gladness" (Ps. 100:2). Consequences: "If you do not obey the voice of the LORD your God…All these curses will come upon you and overtake you…The LORD will send on you cursing, confusion, and rebuke in all you set your hands to do, until you are destroyed and until you perish quickly, because of the wickedness (sexual perversion) of your doings in which you have forsaken Me" (Deut. 28:15-20).

Is there hope for a backslidden America? An America that has gone "Beyond Sodom" in its wickedness (same-sex "marriage") against God and His requirements? Yes, there is hope for America, if it will repent and turn back to God with all its heart. Will America turn? When we experienced 9-11, America turned to God a little, for about one week. Then it went back to its old ways and back to its usual sinful ways. The answer to my question above is found in

Solomon's prayer of dedication of the Temple. God's answer to Solomon was and is:

> "If my people who are called by my name (that includes America) will humble themselves and pray and seek My face, and turn from their wicked ways, then I will hear from heaven, and I will forgive their sin and heal their land" (2 Chronicles 7:14).

America is guilty of committing several major abominations against God. First, America built the new "One World Center" tower in a defiant spirit (Isaiah 9:9-10). They also beamed lights off its spire in rainbow colors, thus co-opting God's sign of mercy and covenant with Noah and mankind, and associating it with the "gay" agenda. President Obama signed the last steel beam to go into the new tower. His words were tantamount to Israel's defiant words in Isaiah 9:10 i.e., "The bricks have fallen, but we will build better and higher." After the tower was completed, its spire was higher than any other spire in the West. It was like Nimrod and his co-workers in Genesis 11:4 who made a rebellious declaration. They said there, "Come let us build ourselves a city a tower that reaches to the heavens, so that we may make a name for ourselves." This is the first overt rebellion against God by a large group in the Bible. This act so moved God that he himself had to come down and avert it, by confusing prideful and rebellious men's tongues! The higher the spire or tower, the greater the pride! Once our Twin Tower Trade Centers were destroyed, the world's tallest buildings were demolished.

Afterwards, the Muslims built the tallest building in the world in the nation of Dubai. Now they are the most prideful nation. Getting back to the second abomination committed by our American leadership, once the Supreme Court of the United States of America signed same sex "marriage" into law, on June 26, 2015; our gay-loving President proceeded to flood the White House, his residence, of the world's greatest nation, with the colors of God's rainbow and sign of mercy, which He gave to Noah and mankind. By his action the President poured salt into America's wound by promoting the gay agenda and the Supreme Court's decision. The so-called gay community co-opted God's rainbow in ignorance and desecrated it. God said in Genesis 9:13, "I have set my bow in the clouds, and it will be the sign of the covenant between me and the earth." I pray that America will heed God's offer (2 Chronicles 7:14) and "humble ourselves and pray and seek God's face and turn from our wicked ways." Only then can God "hear from heaven, forgive our sins and heal our land." The outcome is up to America, its leadership, and the church!

May God have mercy on America.

About the Author

Dr. Aaron B. Claxton has been in Christ for nearly 60 years and has preached the Gospel for nearly 60 years.

Dr. Claxton is the father of seven children, which initially and graciously began with his precious firstborn daughter, Gayle.

He has been married to his lovely wife, Deborah, for nearly 60 years. They are the proud parents of six children (four boys and two girls), all have been called into the five-fold ministry. The Claxtons are also blessed with a host of grandchildren and great grandchildren.

Dr. Claxton's academic background includes earned degrees from Morgan State University, from the Mount Royal College of the Bible and from St. Mary's Seminary and University, where he pursued the academics for the Doctor of Ministry degree. He completed that degree in 1996 at the Family Bible Seminary.

Dr. Claxton has been awarded two honorary Doctorate degrees from Christian International University. They are the Doctor of Divinity and the Doctor of Laws degrees. He received his PhD degree in Biblical Studies from Family Bible Seminary in May 2003.

In addition to this prolific masterpiece, Dr. Claxton has authored over thirty (30) books of which nine (9) others are published (in addition to this one):

1 – *"God's Plan for the Sons of Ham – a future and a hope"*
2 – *"The Biblical View of the Rapture and the Second Coming"*
3 – *"Farrakhan, Islam and Jesus the Messiah"*
4 – *"The Blessing of the Lord is Upon the Tither"*
5 – *"First Fruits the Missing Offering"*
6 – *"Possessing Our Earthly Inheritance Now!"*
7 – *"Caught Up to Meet Him"*
8 – *"Understanding the Root, the Causes and the Remedy of the Middle East Conflict"*
9 – *"ISIS – The Church's Wake Up Call"*

Apostle Claxton, along with his wife, Deborah, founded and pastored the New Creation Christian

Church in Baltimore, Maryland for twenty-three years. He has taught at three Bible Colleges and is well traveled, having preached the Gospel across America and in sixteen nations around the world.

Dr. Claxton stands in the offices of Apostle and Bishop, formally overseeing one hundred plus churches in the U.S., and in East and West Africa, and is presently being established in a global, apostolic ministry, along with his wife, Deborah, in her apostolic ministry. His oldest son, Apostle Aaron Bryan Claxton, along with his wife, Sheila, now pastor the headquarters church in Baltimore, which Dr. Claxton founded in 1968.